Seasons and Colors of the

Appalachian Mountains

Bill L. Booz III

Foreword and Text by Jessy Oberright

Published by Misty Mountain Press
Photography by Bill L. Booz III
www.billbooz.com

Seasons and Colors of the

Appalachian Mountains

Bill L. Booz III

Foreword and Text by Jessy Oberright

Editor: Gene S. Katz
Entire Contents Copyright © Misty Mountain Press 2008
Photographs Copyright © Bill Booz - www.billbooz.com

Published by Misty Mountain Press
114 Great Oak Road
Voorhees, NJ 08043

ISBN 978-0-9767745-1-8

Photographed and Published in the USA. Printed in China.

Front cover: Fog fills the valley before sunrise, Pisgah National Forest, North Carolina.
First frontispiece: Autumn comes to the mountains, Pisgah National Forest, North Carolina.
Back cover: Great Smoky Mountains National Park, Tennessee.

Wind-driven clouds sweep a brilliant autumn valley along the Blue Ridge Parkway, North Carolina.

Sunset reflects on Webb Lake in Maine.

Foreword

The afternoon grew long and the finicky sun played shadow across the mountain peaks and valleys. Bill and I chatted casually as the sun sank lower in the west, gilding the edges of the late day clouds. We both commented on the impending sunset. Though the sky was awash with a quiet purple, the sun was setting unremarkably, gently fading into the oblivion of the night. Absorbed in our own mindless conversation, we crested a ridge. There before us, a brilliant neon sky replaced the dusk. The sudden intensity of the horizon silenced us as we stared speechlessly at the unexpected beauty before us.

The whole event couldn't have lasted more than a minute. It was as if the sky had suddenly flared up, like the embers of a dying fire, only to quietly sputter out. The iridescent glow faded into a deep ocean of young night. It was at that moment, that I realized how fleeting is true beauty. As the freshness of a spring flower, the quiet of new-fallen snow, it lasts a mere second in time.

The Appalachian Mountains have long been revered for their enduring and rugged beauty. Many are called to walk among her green canopies, although few souls possess the perseverance to seek her most sacred of spaces. But for those willing to rise with the sun, endure the bitter cold of her winters, or simply sit in stillness on one of her lofty peaks, nature presents her most precious gift. Turn the page and you will find the amazing beauty of the Appalachian Mountains and her many moods. These pictures enfold you, transporting you to that split second on the mountain crest when the mist settles into the far off valleys just so, and the splendor takes your breath away.

Jessy Oberright

Heavenly morning sunrays highlight the fog-filled valleys in Pisgah National Forest, North Carolina.

Introduction

The Appalachian Mountains, the oldest mountain chain on the continent, began their formation during the Paleozoic Era over 900 million years ago. During the Precambrian Era, some three billion years ago, the Earth entered a time of geological instability which lead to the eventual creation of the Appalachian Mountain range. Over this period, violent forces shaped the Earth transforming the land-masses into one large super-continent called Pangaea.

Pangaea later split apart and continents slowly drifted away from each other. The continents shifted again and began to move back together. As this cycle continued for approximately 400 million years, older mountains were pushed farther west as newer mountains formed, thus creating the seemingly endless ridgelines we see today. They span 1,600 miles in length, as the crow flies, from the Gaspe' Peninsula of Canada to the coastal plain of Alabama, USA.

The excitement from photographing nature often leads me to adventures such as abandoning my white water kayak to the rocks of the Dead River in Maine or being chased by a Black bear in the Blue Ridge Mountains. Maybe it was our trip to Spruce Knob, West Virginia, where I experienced the coldest night of my life in a frost and snow-covered winter wonderland, or our third try to finally find the Ice Caves in Maine, which are only accessible by watercraft, then having to paddle back upstream. It could be summiting a snow-covered mountain peak in Colorado, a road trip across the USA, snowshoeing in New Hampshire, a hot air balloon ride in New Mexico, skiing in Vermont, my 600 RR on any road, viewing a spectacular sunrise, or standing under a glacier-fed waterfall just to feel the cold water soak me instantly. Something about it all just brings me to life.

This book accumulates four years of photographing, putting over 50,000 miles on my vehicles, another 450 miles on my hiking boots, shooting hundreds of rolls of film, and many wonderful adventures that would surpass my wildest dreams.

Even after my spending time in the magnificent Rockies, Cascades, and deserts of the West, the Appalachians still have a special pull that continuously bring me back. Backpacking seven months on the 2,160-mile Appalachian Trail from Georgia to Maine was just a tease, as there are so many beautiful places in the Appalachians, that one could spend a lifetime and still not see it all. I am personally inviting you to share the wonder and beauty that constantly beckon my return to the Appalachian Mountains, in hopes that you too will discover and experience the moments captured in this portfolio, just as I did while photographing "Seasons and Colors of the Appalachian Mountains".

Bill L. Booz III

The sun rises to begin a beautiful day in Shenandoah National Park, Virginia.

The hazy path of the
Appalachian Trail in
Shenandoah National Park,
Virginia winds through a dense
forest of yellow Aster flowers.

Overleaf: Dawn reveals an
endless range of mountains
in Nantahala National Forest,
North Carolina.

A quiet fog lies in the valley at sunrise, Pisgah National Forest, North Carolina.

Morning clouds rise from the valley below the Blue Ridge Parkway, North Carolina.

Fall scene in Nantahala National Forest, North Carolina.

A tree silhouette on a calm lake near Weld, Maine.

Gleaming icicles spill
from the rocks atop
Saddleback Mountain, Maine.

Overleaf: Sunset on
the Appalachian Trail,
Tennessee.

Winter's icy grip holds fast, Green Mountain National Forest, Vermont.

An ocean of clouds fills the valley before sunrise, Jefferson National Forest, Virginia.

Rising vapor creates the blue "smoke" for which these mountains are named. Great Smoky Mountains National Park, Tennessee.

The sun dips below a distant mountain ridge in Pisgah National Forest, North Carolina.

The crescent moon awash in the afterglow of sunset on the Appalachian Trail in Connecticut.

A small creek tumbles through a narrow valley that is beginning to show its first touch of fall color. Pocono Mountains, Pennsylvania.

Dingmans Falls cascades over a rock ledge in the Delaware Water Gap National Recreation Area, Pennsylvania.

Fresh snow coats
Roan Mountain under
a pink-tinged sky in
the Roan Highlands,
Tennessee.

An icy stream cascades
through snow-covered rocks.
Pocono Mountains,
Pennsylvania.

Overleaf: Twilight from
Waterrock Knob,
Blue Ridge Parkway,
North Carolina.

Mountain Laurel blooms in Shenandoah National Park, Virginia.

Brilliant Flame Azalea lights up the ridge along the Appalachian Trail in Tennessee.

Early morning mist lifts to reveal the distant peaks in Chattahoochee National Forest, Georgia.

Rays of light fill the sky along the Blue Ridge Parkway, Virginia.

Clouds recede, thus allowing a
glimpse of trees and a hint of
blue sky in the White
Mountain National Forest,
New Hampshire.

Dragon in the sky -
An unusual cloud formation
along the Appalachian
Trail in Virginia.

Snow dusts the trees and ridges in the Roan Highlands, Tennessee.

Dense clouds lay low in the valleys in winter-bound Killington, Vermont.

Overleaf: Sunrise from the Berkshire Mountains, Massachusetts.

A rainbow appears briefly
in Bridal Veil Falls,
North Carolina.

Cullasaja Falls rushes through an autumn-bedazzled canyon in North Carolina.

A radiant dawn breaks the clouds on Apple Orchard Mountain, Virginia.

A crimson sunrise on Appleton Ridge, Maine.

Fall colors in a rushing stream, Great Smoky Mountains National Park, Tennessee.

Autumn maples wash the hillside in a pallet of brilliant color on the Blue Ridge Parkway, North Carolina.

Early dawn on the
Appalachian Trail,
Shenandoah National
Park, Virginia.

Star of Sunrise -
Clingmans Dome,
Great Smoky Mountains
National Park, Tennessee.

Dunnfield Creek twists playfully through the Delaware Water Gap National Recreation Area, New Jersey.

Vast fields of clouds hang in the valley floor, Pisgah National Forest, North Carolina.

A Monarch butterfly perches on a milkweed plant, Shenandoah National Park, Virginia.

A blue damselfly clings to a reed, Delaware Water Gap National Recreation Area, Pennsylvania.

Majestic Bald eagles along the river banks in New York.

A Spiderwort on Cold Mountain in Virginia.

A yellow Lady's Slipper,
Shenandoah National Park,
Virginia.

Overleaf: A crystal palace of
snowladen trees endures
winter's harsh grasp in the
Bigelow Preserve, Maine.

Wispy clouds gather around the mountains, Blue Ridge Parkway, North Carolina.

Fog-filled valleys and fall-colored mountains, Pisgah National Forest, North Carolina.

About the Photographer

Bill's photographic adventures started during his 1999 through-hike of the Appalachian Trail, a 2,160-mile long footpath that extends from Springer Mountain, Georgia to Mt. Katahdin, Maine. His seven-month journey took him through 14 states, up and down many mountains, and is the equivalent of climbing Mt. Everest many times over. Since the journey, Bill, known as Orion in the hiking community, has continued to scout the Appalachian Mountains and beyond to find and capture beautiful moments to share with you.

Fine art prints, calendars and post-cards, are available for sale at www.billbooz.com or by writing to: Misty Mountain Press 114 Great Oak Road Voorhees, NJ 08043.